DYMER

"Nine nights I hung upon the Tree, wounded with the spear, as an offering to Odin, myself sacrificed to myself."—Havamal.

DYMER

by C. S. Lewis

CANTO I

1

You stranger, long before your glance can light
Upon these words, time will have washed away
The moment when I first took pen to write,
With all my road before me—yet to-day,
Here, if at all, we meet; the unfashioned clay
Ready to both our hands; both hushed to see
That which is nowhere yet come forth and be.

2

This moment, if you join me, we begin
A partnership where both must toil to hold
The clue that I caught first. We lose or win
Together; if you read, you are enrolled.
And first, a marvel—Who could have foretold
That in the city which men called in scorn
The Perfect City, Dymer could be born?

3

There you'd have thought the gods were smothered down
Forever, and the keys were turned on fate.
No hour was left unchartered in that town,
And love was in a schedule and the State
Chose for eugenic reasons who should mate
With whom, and when. Each idle song and dance
Was fixed by law and nothing left to chance.

4

For some of the last Platonists had founded
That city of old. And mastery they made
An island of what ought to be, surrounded
By this gross world of easier light and shade.
All answering to the master's dream they laid
The strong foundations, torturing into stone
Each bubble that the Academy had blown.

5

This people were so pure, so law-abiding,
So logical, they made the heavens afraid:
They sent the very swallows into hiding
By their appalling chastity dismayed:
More soberly the lambs in springtime played
Because of them: and ghosts dissolved in shame
Before their common-sense—till Dymer came.

6

At Dymer's birth no comets scared the nation,
The public crèche engulfed him with the rest,
And twenty separate Boards of Education
Closed round him. He was passed through every test,
Was vaccinated, numbered, washed and dressed,
Proctored, inspected, whipt, examined weekly,
And for some nineteen years he bore it meekly.

7

For nineteen years they worked upon his soul,
Refining, chipping, moulding and adorning.
Then came the moment that undid the whole—
The ripple of rude life without a warning.
It came in lecture-time one April morning
—Alas for laws and locks, reproach and praise,
Who ever learned to censor the spring days?

8

A little breeze came stirring to his cheek.
He looked up to the window. A brown bird
Perched on the sill, bent down to whet his beak
With darting head—Poor Dymer watched and stirred
Uneasily. The lecturer's voice he heard
Still droning from the dais. The narrow room

Was drowsy, over-solemn, filled with gloom.

9

He yawned, and a voluptuous laziness
Tingled down all his spine and loosed his knees,
Slow-drawn, like an invisible caress.
He laughed—The lecturer stopped like one that sees
A Ghost, then frowned and murmured, "Silence, please."
That moment saw the soul of Dymer hang
In the balance—Louder then his laughter rang.

10

The whole room watched with unbelieving awe,
He rose and staggered rising. From his lips
Broke yet again the idiot-like guffaw.
He felt the spirit in his finger-tips,
Then swinging his right arm—a wide ellipse
Yet lazily—he struck the lecturer's head.
The old man tittered, lurched and dropt down dead.

11

Out of the silent room, out of the dark
Into the sum-stream Dymer passed, and there
The sudden breezes, the high hanging lark
The milk-white clouds sailing in polished air,
Suddenly flashed about him like a blare
Of trumpets. And no cry was raised behind him.
His class sat dazed. They dared not go to find him.

12

Yet wonderfully some rumour spread abroad—
An inarticulate sense of life renewing
In each young heart—He whistled down the road:
Men said: "There's Dymer"—"Why, what's Dymer doing?"

DYMER

"I don't know"–"Look, there's Dymer,"–far pursuing
With troubled eyes–A long mysterious "Oh"
Sighed from a hundred throats to see him go.

13

Down the white street and past the gate and forth
Beyond the wall he came to grassy places.
There was a shifting wind to West and North
With clouds in heeling squadron running races.
The shadows following on the sunlight's traces
Crossed the whole field and each wild flower within it
With change of wavering glories every minute.

14

There was a river, flushed with rains, between
The flat fields and a forest's willowy edge.
A sauntering pace he shuffled on the green,
He kicked his boots against the crackly sedge
And tore his hands in many a furzy hedge.
He saw his feet and ankles gilded round
With buttercups that carpeted the ground.

15

He looked back then. The line of a low hill
Had hid the city's towers and domes from sight;
He stopt: he felt a break of sunlight spill
Around him sudden waves of searching light.
Upon the earth was green, and gold, and white
Smothering his feet. He felt his city dress
An insult to that April cheerfulness.

16

He said: "I've worn this dust heap long enough,
Here goes!" And forthwith in the open field

C. S. Lewis

He stripped away that prison of sad stuff:
Socks, jacket, shirt and breeches off he peeled
And rose up mother-naked with no shield
Against the sun: then stood awhile to play
With bare toes dabbling in cold river clay.

17

Forward again, and sometimes leaping high
With arms outspread as though he would embrace
In one act all the circle of the sky:
Sometimes he rested in a leafier place,
And crushed the wet, cool flowers against his face:
And once he cried aloud, "Oh world, oh day,
Let, let me,"—and then found no prayer to say.

18

Up furrows still unpierced with earliest crop
He marched. Through woods he strolled from flower to flower,
And over hills. As ointment drop by drop
Preciously meted out, so hour by hour
The day slipped through his hands: and now the power
Failed in his feet from walking. He was done,
Hungry and cold. That moment sank the sun.

19

He lingered—Looking up, he saw ahead
The black and bristling frontage of a wood
And over it the large sky swimming red
Freckled with homeward crows. Surprised he stood
To feel that wideness quenching his hot mood,
Then shouted, "Trembling darkness, trembling green,
What do you mean, wild wood, what do you mean?"

20

He shouted. But the solitude received
His noise into her noiselessness, his fire
Into her calm. Perhaps he half believed
Some answer yet would come to his desire.
The hushed air quivered softly like a wire
Upon his voice. It echoed, it was gone:
The quiet and the quiet dark went on.

21

He rushed into the wood. He struck and stumbled
On hidden roots. He groped and scratched his face.
The little birds woke chattering where he fumbled.
The stray cat stood, paw lifted, in mid-chase.
There is a windless calm in such a place.
A sense of being indoors—so crowded stand
The living trees, watching on every hand:

22

A sense of trespass—such as in the hall
Of the wrong house, one time, to me befell.
Groping between the hatstand and the wall—
A clear voice from above me like a bell,
The sweet voice of a woman asking "Well?"
No more than this. And as I fled I wondered
Into whose alien story I had blundered.

23

A like thing fell to Dymer. Bending low,
Feeling his way he went. The curtained air
Sighed into sound above his head, as though
Stringed instruments and horns were riding there.
It passed and at its passing stirred his hair.
He stood intent to hear. He heard again
And checked his breath half-drawn, as if with pain.

C. S. Lewis

24

That music could have crumbled proud belief
With doubt, or in the bosom of the sage
Madden the heart that had outmastered grief,
And flood with tears the eyes of frozen age
And turn the young man's feet to pilgrimage—
So sharp it was, so sure a path it found,
Soulward with stabbing wounds of bitter sound.

25

It died out on the middle of a note,
As though it failed at the urge of its own meaning.
It left him with life quivering at the throat,
Limbs shaken and wet cheeks and body leaning,
With strain towards the sound and senses gleaning
The last, least, ebbing ripple of the air,
Searching the emptied darkness, muttering "Where?"

26

Then followed such a time as is forgotten
With morning light, but in the passing seems
Unending. Where he grasped the branch was rotten,
Where he trod forth in haste the forest streams
Laid wait for him. Like men in fever dreams
Climbing an endless rope, he laboured much
And gained no ground. He reached and could not touch.

27

And often out of darkness like a swell
That grows up from no wind upon blue sea,
He heard the music, unendurable
In stealing sweetness wind from tree to tree.
Battered and bruised in body and soul was he
When first he saw a little lightness growing

11

Ahead: and from that light the sound was flowing.

28
The trees were fewer now: and gladly nearing
That light, he saw the stars. For sky was there,
And smoother grass, white flowered—a forest clearing
Set in seven miles of forest, secreter
Than valleys in the tops of clouds, more fair
Than greenery under snow or desert water
Or the white peace descending after slaughter.

29
As some who have been wounded beyond healing
Wake, or half wake, once only and so bless
Far off the lamplight travelling on the ceiling.
A disk of pale light filled with peacefulness
And wonder if this is the C.C.S.,
Or home, or heaven, or dreams—then sighing win
Wise, ignorant death before the pains begin:

30
So Dymer in the wood-lawn blessed the light,
A still light, rosy, clear, and filled with sound.
Here was some pile of building which the night
Made larger. Spiry shadows rose all round,
But through the open door appeared profound
Recesses of pure light—fire with no flame—
And out of that deep light the music came.

31
Tip-toes he slunk towards it where the grass
Was twinkling in a lane of light before
The archway. There was neither fence to pass
Nor word of challenge given, nor bolted door,

But where it's open, open evermore,
No knocker and no porter and no guard,
For very strangeness entering in grows hard.

32

Breathe not! Speak not! Walk gently. Someone's here,
Why have they left their house with the door so wide?
There must be someone.... Dymer hung in fear
Upon the threshold, longing and big-eyed.
At last he squared his shoulders, smote his side
And called, "I'm here. Now let the feast begin.
I'm coming now. I'm Dymer," and went in.

CANTO II

1

More light. Another step, and still more light
Opening ahead. It swilled with soft excess,
His eyes yet quivering from the dregs of night,
And it was nowhere more and nowhere less:
In it no shadows were. He could not guess
Its fountain. Wondering round around he turned:
Still on each side the level glory burned.

2

Far in the dome to where his gaze was lost
The deepening roof shone clear as stones that lie
In-shore beneath pure seas. The aisles, that crossed
Like forests of white stone their arms on high,
Past pillar after pillar dragged his eye
In unobscured perspective till the sight
Was weary. And there also was the light.

3

Look with my eyes. Conceive yourself above

DYMER

And hanging in the dome: and thence through space
Look down. See Dymer, dwarfed and naked, move,
A white blot on the floor, at such a pace
As boats that hardly seem to have changed place
Once in an hour when from the cliffs we spy
The same ship always smoking towards the sky.

4
The shouting mood had withered from his heart;
The oppression of huge places wrapped him round.
A great misgiving sent its fluttering dart
Deep into him—some fear of being found,
Some hope to find he knew not what. The sound
Of music, never ceasing, took the rôle
Of silence and like silence numbed his soul.

5
Till, as he turned a corner, his deep awe
Broke with a sudden start. For straight ahead,
Far off, a wild eyed, naked man he saw
That came to meet him: and beyond was spread
Yet further depth of light. With quickening tread
He leaped towards the shape. Then stopped and smiled
Before a mirror, wondering like a child.

6
Beside the glass, unguarded, for the claiming,
Like a great patch of flowers upon the wall
Hung every kind of clothes: silk, feathers flaming,
Leopard skin, furry mantles like the fall
Of deep mid-winter snows. Upon them all
Hung the faint smell of cedar, and the dyes
Were bright as blood and clear as morning skies.

C. S. Lewis

7

He turned from the white spectre in the glass
And looked at these. Remember, he had worn
Thro' winter slush, thro' summer flowers and grass
One kind of solemn stuff since he was born,
With badge of year and rank. He laughed in scorn
And cried, "Here is no law, nor eye to see,
Nor leave of entry given. Why should there be?

8

"Have done with that—you threw it all behind.
Henceforth I ask no licence where I need.
It's on, on, on, though I go mad and blind,
Though knees ache and lungs labour and feet bleed,
Or else—it's home again: to sleep and feed,
And work, and hate them always and obey
And loathe the punctual rise of each new day."

9

He made mad work among them as he dressed,
With motley choice and litter on the floor,
And each thing as he found it seemed the best.
He wondered that he had not known before
How fair a man he was. "I'll creep no more
In secret," Dymer said. "But I'll go back
And drive them all to freedom on this track."

10

He turned towards the glass. The space looked smaller
Behind him now. Himself in royal guise
Filled the whole frame—a nobler shape and taller,
Till suddenly he started with surprise,
Catching, by chance, his own familiar eyes,
Fevered, yet still the same, without their share

DYMER

Of bravery, undeceived and watching there.

11

Yet, as he turned, he cried, "The rest remain....
If they rebelled ... if they should find me here,
We'd pluck the whole taut fabric from the strain,
Hew down the city, let live earth appear!
—Old men and barren women whom through fear
We have suffered to be masters in our home,
Hide! hide! for we are angry and we come."

12

Thus feeding on vain fancy, covering round
His hunger, his great loneliness arraying
In facile dreams until the qualm was drowned,
The boy went on. Through endless arches straying
With casual tread he sauntered, manly playing
At manhood lest more loss of faith betide him,
Till lo! he saw a table set beside him.

13

When Dymer saw this sight, he leaped for mirth,
He clapped his hands, his eye lit like a lover's.
He had a hunger in him that was worth
Ten cities. Here was silver, glass and covers.
Cold peacock, prauns in aspic, eggs of plovers,
Raised pies that stood like castles, gleaming fishes
And bright fruit with broad leaves around the dishes.

14

If ever you have passed a café door
And lingered in the dusk of a June day,
Fresh from the road, sweat-sodden and foot-sore,
And heard the plates clink and the music play,

With laughter, with white tables far away,
With many lights—conceive how Dymer ran
To table, looked once round him, and began.

15

That table seemed unending. Here and there
Were broken meats, bread crumbled, flowers defaced
—A napkin, with white petals, on a chair,
—A glass already tasted, still to taste.
It seemed that a great host had fed in haste
And gone: yet left a thousand places more
Untouched, wherein no guest had sat before.

16

There in the lonely splendour Dymer ate,
As thieves eat, ever watching, half in fear.
He blamed his evil fortune. "I come late.
Whose board was this? What company sat here?
What women with wise mouths, what comrades dear
Who would have made me welcome as the one
Free-born of all my race and cried, 'Well done!'"

17

Remember, yet again, he had grown up
On rations and on scientific food,
At common boards, with water in his cup,
One mess alike for every day and mood:
But here, at his right hand, a flagon stood.
He raised it, paused before he drank, and laughed.
"I'll drown their Perfect City in this draught."

18

He fingered the cold neck. He saw within,
Like a strange sky, some liquor that foamed blue

And murmured. Standing now with pointed chin
And head thrown back, he tasted. Rapture flew
Through every vein. That moment louder grew
The music and swelled forth a trumpet note.
He ceased and put one hand up to his throat.

19
Then heedlessly he let the flagon sink
In his right hand. His staring eyes were caught
In distance, as of one who tries to think
A thought that is still waiting to be thought.
There was a riot in his heart that brought
The loud blood to the temples. A great voice
Sprang to his lips unsummoned, with no choice.

20
"Ah! but the eyes are open, the dream is broken!
To sack the Perfect City?... a fool's deed
For Dymer! Folly of follies I have spoken!
I am the wanderer, new born, newly freed....
A thousand times they have warned me of men's greed
For joy, for the good that all desire, but never
Till now I knew the wild heat of the endeavour.

21
"Some day I will come back to break the City,
—Not now. Perhaps when age is white and bleak
—Not now. I am in haste. Oh God, the pity
Of all my life till this, groping and weak,
The shadow of itself! But now to seek
That true most ancient glory whose white glance
Was lost through the whole world by evil chance!

22

"I was a dull, cowed thing from the beginning.
Dymer the drudge, the blackleg who obeyed.
Desire shall teach me now. If this be sinning,
Good luck to it! Oh splendour long delayed,
Beautiful world of mine, oh world arrayed
For bridal, flower and forest, wave and field,
I come to be your lover. Loveliest, yield!

23

"World, I will prove you. Lest it should be said
There was a man who loved the earth: his heart
Was nothing but that love. With doting tread
He worshipt the loved grass: and every start
Of every bird from cover, the least part
Of every flower he held in awe. Yet earth
Gave him no joy between his death and birth.

24

"I know my good is hidden at your breast.
There is a sound of great good in my ear,
Like wings. And, oh! this moment is the best;
I shall not fail—I taste it—it comes near.
As men from a dark dungeon see the clear
Stars shining and the filled streams far away,
I hear your promise booming and obey.

25

"This forest lies a thousand miles, perhaps,
Beyond where I am come. And farther still
The rivers wander seaward with smooth lapse,
And there is cliff and cottage, tower and hill.
Somewhere, before the world's end, I shall fill
My spirit at earth's pap. For earth must hold

DYMER

One rich thing sealed as Dymer's from of old.

26
"One rich thing—or, it may be, more than this....
Might I not reach the borders of a land
That ought to have been mine? And there, the bliss
Of free speech, there the eyes that understand,
The men free grown, not modelled by the hand
Of masters—men that know, or men that seek,
—They will not gape and murmur when I speak."

27
Then, as he ceased, amid the farther wall
He saw a curtained and low lintelled door;
—Dark curtains, sweepy fold, night-purple pall,
He thought he had not noticed it before.
Sudden desire for darkness overbore
His will, and drew him towards it. All was blind
Within. He passed. The curtains closed behind.

28
He entered in a void. Night-scented flowers
Breathed there, but this was darker than the night
That is most black with beating thundershowers,
—A disembodied world where depth and height
And distance were unmade. No seam of light
Showed through. It was a world not made for seeing,
One pure, one undivided sense of being.

29
Through darkness smooth as amber, warily, slowly
He moved. The floor was soft beneath his feet.
A cool smell that was holy and unholy,
Sharp like the very spring and roughly sweet

20

Blew towards him: and he felt his fingers meet
Broad leaves and wiry stems that at his will
Unclosed before and closed behind him still.

30

With body intent he felt the foliage quiver
On breast and thighs. With groping arms he made
Wide passes in the air. A sacred shiver
Of joy from the heart's centre oddly strayed
To every nerve. Deep sighing, much afraid,
Much wondering, he went on: then, stooping, found
A knee-depth of warm pillows on the ground.

31

And there it was sweet rapture to lie still,
Eyes open on the dark. A flowing health
Bathed him from head to foot and great goodwill
Rose springing in his heart and poured its wealth
Outwards. Then came a hand as if by stealth
Out of the dark and touched his hand: and after
The beating silence budded into laughter:

32

—A low grave laugh and rounded like a pearl,
Mysterious, filled with home. He opened wide
His arms. The breathing body of a girl
Slid into them. From the world's end, with the stride
Of seven league boots came passion to his side.
Then, meeting mouths, soft-falling hair, a cry,
Heart-shaken flank, sudden cool-folded thigh:

33

The same night swelled the mushroom in earth's lap
And silvered the wet fields: it drew the bud

From hiding and led on the rhythmic sap
And sent the young wolves thirsting after blood,
And, wheeling the big seas, made ebb and flood
Along the shores of earth: and held these two
In dead sleep till the time of morning dew.

CANTO III

1

He woke, and all at once before his eyes
The pale spires of the chestnut-trees in bloom
Rose waving and, beyond, dove-coloured skies;
But where he lay was dark and, out of gloom,
He saw them, through the doorway of a room
Full of strange scents and softness, padded deep
With growing leaves, heavy with last night's sleep.

2

He rubbed his eyes. He felt that chamber wreathing
New sleepiness around him. At his side
He was aware of warmth and quiet breathing.
Twice he sank back, loose limbed and drowsy eyed;
But the wind came even there. A sparrow cried
And the wood shone without. Then Dymer rose,
—"Just for one glance," he said, and went, tip-toes,

3

Out into crisp grey air and drenching grass.
The whitened cobweb sparkling in its place
Clung to his feet. He saw the wagtail pass
Beside him and the thrush: and from his face
Felt the thin-scented winds divinely chase
The flush of sleep. Far off he saw, between
The trees, long morning shadows of dark green.

C. S. Lewis

4

He stretched his lazy arms to their full height,
Yawning, and sighed and laughed, and sighed anew:
Then wandered farther, watching with delight
How his broad naked footprints stained the dew,
—Pressing his foot to feel the cold come through
Between the spreading toes—then wheeling round
Each moment to some new, shrill forest sound.

5

The wood with its cold flowers had nothing there
More beautiful than he, new waked from sleep,
New born from joy. His soul lay very bare
That moment to life's touch, and pondering deep
Now first he knew that no desire could keep
These hours for always, and that men do die
—But oh, the present glory of lungs and eye!

6

He thought: "At home they are waking now. The stair
Is filled with feet. The bells clang—far from me.
Where am I now? I could not point to where
The City lies from here," ... then, suddenly,
"If I were here alone, these woods could be
A frightful place! But now I have met my friend
Who loves me, we can talk to the road's end."

7

Thus, quickening with the sweetness of the tale
Of his new love, he turned. He saw, between
The young leaves where the palace walls showed pale
With chilly stone: but far above the green,
Springing like cliffs in air, the towers were seen,
Making more quiet yet the quiet dawn.

Thither he came. He reached the open lawn.

8

No bird was moving here. Against the wall
Out of the unscythed grass the nettle grew.
The doors stood open wide, but no footfall
Rang in the colonnades. Whispering through
Arches and hollow halls the light wind blew....
His awe returned. He whistled—then, no more,
It's better to plunge in by the first door.

9

But then the vastness threw him into doubt.
Was this the door that he had found last night?
Or that, beneath the tower? Had he come out
This side at all? As the first snow falls light
With following rain before the year grows white,
So the first, dim foreboding touched his mind,
Gently as yet, and easily thrust behind.

10

And with it came the thought, "I do not know
Her name—no, nor her face." But still his mood
Ran blithely as he felt the morning blow
About him, and the earth-smell in the wood
Seemed waking for long hours that must be good
Here, in the unfettered lands, that knew no cause
For grudging—out of reach of the old laws.

11

He hastened to one entry. Up the stair,
Beneath the pillared porch, without delay,
He ran—then halted suddenly: for there
Across the quiet threshold something lay,

C. S. Lewis

A bundle, a dark mass that barred the way.
He looked again and lo, the formless pile
Under his eyes was moving all the while.

12

And it had hands, pale hands of wrinkled flesh,
Puckered and gnarled with vast antiquity,
That moved. He eyed the sprawling thing afresh,
And bit by bit (so faces come to be
In the red coal) yet surely, he could see
That the swathed hugeness was uncleanly human,
A living thing, the likeness of a woman.

13

In the centre a draped hummock marked the head;
Thence flowed the broader lines with curve and fold
Spreading as oak roots do. You would have said
A man could hide among them and grow old
In finding a way out. Breasts manifold
As of the Ephesian Artemis might be
Under that robe. The face he did not see.

14

And all his being answered, "Not that way!"
Never a word he spoke. Stealthily creeping
Back from the door he drew. Quick! No delay!
Quick, quick, but very quiet!—backward peeping
Till fairly out of sight. Then shouting, leaping,
Shaking himself he ran—as puppies do
From bathing—till that door was out of view.

15

Another gate—and empty. In he went
And found a courtyard open to the sky

DYMER

Amidst it dripped a fountain. Heavy scent
Of flowers was here; the foxglove standing high
Sheltered the whining wasp. With hasty eye
He travelled round the walls. One doorway led
Within: one showed a further court ahead.

16
He ran up to the first—a hungry lover,
And not yet taught to endure, not blunted yet,
But weary of long waiting to discover
That loved one's face. Before his foot was set
On the first stair, he felt the sudden sweat,
Cold on his sides. That sprawling mass in view,
That shape—the horror of heaviness—here too.

17
He fell back from the porch. Not yet—not yet—
There must be other ways where he would meet
No watcher in the door. He would not let
The fear rise, nor hope falter, nor defeat
Be entered in his thoughts. A sultry heat
Seemed to have filled the day. His breath came short,
And he passed on into that inner court.

18
And (like a dream) the sight he feared to find
Was waiting here. Then cloister, path and square
He hastened through: down paths that needed blind,
Traced and retraced his steps. The thing sat there
In every door, still watching, everywhere,
Behind, ahead, all round—So! Steady now,
Lest panic comes. He stopped. He wiped his brow.

19

But, as he strove to rally, came the thought
That he had dreamed of such a place before
—Knew how it all would end. He must be caught
Early or late. No good! But all the more
He raged with passionate will that overbore
That knowledge: and cried out, and beat his head,
Raving, upon the senseless walls, and said,

20

"Where? Where? Dear, look once out. Give but one sign.
It's I, I, Dymer. Are you chained and hidden?
What have they done to her? Loose her! She is mine.
Through stone and iron, haunted and hag-ridden,
I'll come to you—no stranger, nor unbidden,
It's I. Don't fear them. Shout above them all.
Can you not hear? I'll follow at your call."

21

From every arch the echo of his cry
Returned. Then all was silent, and he knew
There was no other way. He must pass by
That horror: tread her down, force his way through,
Or die upon the threshold. And this too
Had all been in a dream. He felt his heart
Beating as if his throat would burst apart.

22

There was no other way. He stood a space
And pondered it. Then, gathering up his will,
He went to the next door. The pillared place
Beneath the porch was dark. The air was still,
Moss on the steps. He felt her presence fill
The threshold with dull life. Here too was she.

This time he raised his eyes and dared to see.

23

Pah! Only an old woman!... but the size,
The old, old matriarchal dreadfulness,
Immoveable, intolerable ... the eyes
Hidden, the hidden head, the winding dress
Corpselike.... The weight of the brute that seemed to press
Upon his heart and breathing. Then he heard
His own voice, strange and humbled, take the word.

24

"Good Mother, let me pass. I have a friend
To look for in this house. I slept the night
And feasted here—it was my journey's end,
—I found it by the music and the light,
And no one kept the doors, and I did right
To enter—did I not? Now, Mother, pray,
Let me pass in ... good Mother, give me way."

25

The woman answered nothing: but he saw
The hands, like crabs, still wandering on her knee.
"Mother, if I have broken any law,
I'll ask a pardon once: then let it be,
—Once is enough—and leave the passage free.
I am in haste. And though it were a sin
By all the laws you have, I must go in."

26

Courage was rising in him now. He said,
"Out of my path, old woman. For this cause
I am new born, new freed, and here new wed,
That I might be the breaker of bad laws.

The frost of old forbiddings breaks and thaws
Wherever my feet fall. I bring to birth
Under its crust the green, ungrudging earth."

27

He had started, bowing low: but now he stood
Stretched to his height. His own voice in his breast
Made misery pompous, firing all his blood.
"Enough," he cried. "Give place. You shall not wrest
My love from me. I journey on a quest
You cannot understand, whose strength shall bear me
Through fire and earth. A bogy will not scare me.

28

"I am the sword of spring; I am the truth.
Old night put out your stars, the dawn is here,
The sleeper's wakening, and the wings of youth.
With crumbling veneration and cowed fear
I make no truce. My loved one, live and dear,
Waits for me. Let me in! I fled the City,
Shall I fear you or ... Mother, ah, for pity."

29

For his high mood fell shattered. Like a man
Unnerved, in bayonet-fighting, in the thick,
—Full of red rum and cheers when he began,
Now, in a dream, muttering: "I've not the trick.
It's no good. I'm no good. They're all too quick.
There! Look there! Look at that!" So Dymer stood,
Suddenly drained of hope. It was no good.

30

He pleaded then. Shame beneath shame. "Forgive.
It may be there are powers I cannot break.

If you are of them, speak. Speak. Let me live.
I ask so small a thing. I beg. I make
My body a living prayer whose force would shake
The mountains. I'll recant—confess my sin—
But this once let me pass. I must go in.

31

"Yield but one inch, once only from your law
Set any price—I will give all, obey
All else but this, hold your least word in awe,
Give you no cause for anger from this day.
Answer! The least things living when they pray
As I pray now bear witness. They speak true
Against God. Answer! Mother, let me through."

32

Then when he heard no answer, mad with fear
And with desire, too strained with both to know
What he desired or feared, yet staggering near,
He forced himself towards her and bent low
For grappling. Then came darkness. Then a blow
Fell on his heart, he thought. There came a blank
Of all things. As the dead sink, down he sank.

33

The first big drops are rattling on the trees,
The sky is copper dark, low thunder pealing.
See Dymer with drooped head and knocking knees
Comes from the porch. Then slowly, drunkly reeling,
Blind, beaten, broken, past desire of healing,
Past knowledge of his misery, he goes on
Under the first dark trees and now is gone.

CANTO IV

1

First came the peal that split the heavens apart
Straight overhead. Then silence. Then the rain;
Twelve miles of downward water like one dart,
And in one leap were launched along the plain,
To break the budding flower and flood the grain,
And keep with dripping sound an undersong
Amid the wheeling thunder all night long.

2

He put his hands before his face. He stooped
Blind with his hair. The loud drops' grim tattoo
Beat him to earth. Like summer grass he drooped,
Amazed, while sheeted lightning large and blue
Blinked wide and pricked the quivering eyeball through.
Then, scrambling to his feet, with downward head
He fought into the tempest as chance led.

3

The wood was mad. Soughing of branch and straining
Was there: drumming of water. Light was none
Nor knowledge of himself. The trees' complaining
And his own throbbing heart seemed mixed in one,
One sense of bitter loss and beauty undone;
All else was blur and chaos and rain-steam
And noise and the confusion of a dream.

4

Aha!... Earth hates a miserable man:
Against him even the clouds and winds conspire.
Heaven's voice smote Dymer's ear-drum as he ran,
Its red throat plagued the dark with corded fire
—Barbed flame, coiled flame that ran like living wire

DYMER

Charged with disastrous current, left and right
About his path, hell-blue or staring white.

5
Stab! Stab! Blast all at once. What's he to fear?
Look there—that cedar shrivelling in swift blight
Even where he stood! And there—ah, that came near!
Oh, if some shaft would break his soul outright,
What ease so to unload and scatter quite
On the darkness this wild beating in his skull,
Too burning to endure, too tense and full.

6
All lost: and driven away: even her name
Unknown. O fool, to have wasted for a kiss
Time when they could have talked! An angry shame
Was in him. He had worshipt earth, and this
—The venomed clouds fire spitting from the abyss,
This was the truth indeed, the world's intent
Unmasked and naked now, the thing it meant.

7
The storm lay on the forest a great time
—Wheeled in its thundery circuit, turned, returned.
Still through the dead-leaved darkness, through the slime
Of standing pools and slots of clay storm-churned
Went Dymer. Still the knotty lightning burned
Along black air. He heard the unbroken sound
Of water rising in the hollower ground.

8
He cursed it in his madness, flung it back,
Sorrow as wild as young men's sorrows are,
Till, after midnight, when the tempest's track

Drew off, between two clouds appeared one star.
Then his mood changed. And this was heavier far,
When bit by bit, rarer and still more rare,
The weakening thunder ceased from the cleansed air;

9

When leaves began to drip with dying rain
And trees showed black against the glimmering sky,
When the night-birds flapped out and called again
Above him: when the silence cool and shy
Came stealing to its own, and streams ran by
Now audible amid the rustling wood
—Oh, then came the worst hour for flesh and blood.

10

It was no nightmare now with fiery stream
Too horrible to last, able to blend
Itself and all things in one hurrying dream;
It was the waking world that will not end
Because hearts break, that is not foe nor friend,
Where sane and settled knowledge first appears
Of workday desolation, with no tears.

11

He halted then, foot-sore, weary to death
And heard his heart beating in solitude,
When suddenly the sound of sharpest breath
Indrawn with pain and the raw smell of blood
Surprised his sense. Near by to where he stood
Came a long whimpering moan—a broken word,
A rustle of leaves where some live body stirred.

12

He groped towards the sound. "What, brother, brother,

DYMER

Who groaned?"—"I'm hit. I'm finished. Let me be."
—"Put out your hand, then. Reach me. No, the other."
—"Don't touch. Fool! Damn you. Leave me."—"I can't see.
Where are you?" Then more groans. "They've done for me.
I've no hands. Don't come near me. No, but stay,
Don't leave me ... oh my God! Is it near day?"

13
—"Soon now, a little longer. Can you sleep?
I'll watch for you."—"Sleep, is it? That's ahead,
But none till then. Listen, I've bled too deep
To last out till the morning. I'll be dead
Within the hour—sleep then. I've heard it said
They don't mind at the last, but this is Hell.
If I'd the strength—I have such things to tell."

14
All trembling in the dark and sweated over
Like a man reared in peace, unused to pain,
Sat Dymer near him in the lightless cover,
Afraid to touch and shamefaced to refrain.

Then bit by bit and often checked again
With agony the voice told on. (The place
Was dark, that neither saw the other's face.)

15
"There is a City which men call in scorn
The Perfect City—eastward of this wood—
You've heard about the place. There I was born.
I'm one of them, their work. Their sober mood,
The ordered life, the laws, are in my blood
—A life ... well, less than happy, something more
Than the red greed and lusts that went before.

34

16

"All in one day one man and at one blow
Brought ruin on us all. There was a boy
—Blue eyes, large limbs, were all he had to show,
You need no greater prophets to destroy.
He seemed a man asleep. Sorrow and joy
Had passed him by—the dreamiest, safest man,
The most obscure, until this curse began.

17

"Then—how or why it was, I cannot say,
This Dymer, this fool baby pink-and-white,
Went mad beneath his quiet face. One day,
With nothing said, he rose and laughed outright
Before his master: then, in all our sight,
Even where we sat to watch, he struck him dead
And screamed with laughter once again and fled.

18

"Lord! how it all comes back. How still the place is,
And he there lying dead ... only the sound
Of a bluebottle buzzing ... sharpened faces
Strained, gaping from the benches all around...
The dead man hunched and quiet with no wound,
And minute after minute terror creeping
With dreadful hopes to set the wild heart leaping.

19

"Then one by one at random (no word spoken),
We slipt out to the sunlight and away.
We felt the empty sense of something broken
And comfortless adventure all that day.
Men loitered at their work and could not say
What trembled at their lips or what new light

DYMER

Was in girls' eyes. Yet we endured till night.

20
"Then ... I was lying wide awake in bed,
Shot through with tremulous thought, lame hopes, and sweet
Desire of reckless days—with burning head.
And then there came a clamour from the street,
Came nearer, nearer, nearer—stamping feet
And screaming song and curses and a shout
Of 'Who's for Dymer, Dymer?—Up and out!'

21
"We looked out from our window. Thronging there
A thousand of our people, girls and men,
Raved and reviled and shouted by the glare
Of torches and of bonfire blaze. And then
Came tumult from the street beyond: again
'Dymer' they cried. And farther off there came
The sound of gun-fire and the gleam of flame.

22
"I rushed down with the rest. Oh, we were mad!
After this, it's all nightmare. The black sky
Between the housetops framed was all we had
To tell us that the old world could not die
And that we were no gods. The flood ran high
When first I came, but after was the worse,
Oh, to recall...! On Dymer rest the curse!

23
"Our leader was a hunchback with red hair
—Bran was his name. He had that kind of force
About him that will hold your eyes fast there
As in ten miles of green one patch of gorse

36

Will hold them—do you know? His lips were coarse
But his eyes like a prophet's—seemed to fill
The whole face. And his tongue was never still.

24

"He cried: 'As Dymer broke, we'll break the chain.
The world is free. They taught you to be chaste
And labour and bear orders and refrain.
Refrain? From what? All's good enough. We'll taste
Whatever is. Life murmurs from the waste
Beneath the mind ... who made the reasoning part
The jailer of the wild gods in the heart?'

25

"We were a ragtail crew—wild-haired, half dressed,
All shouting, 'Up, for Dymer! Up away!'
Yet each one always watching all the rest
And looking to his back. And some were gay
Like drunk men, some were cringing, pinched and grey
With terror dry on the lip. (The older ones
Had had the sense enough to bring their guns.)

26

"The wave where I was swallowed swelled and broke,
After long surge, into the open square.
And here there was more light: new clamour woke.
Here first I heard the bullets sting the air
And went hot round the heart. Our lords were there
In barricade with all their loyal men.
For every one man loyal Bran led ten.

27

"Then charge and cheer and bubbling sobs of death,
We hovered on their front. Like swarming bees

Their spraying bullets came—no time for breath.
I saw men's stomachs fall out on their knees;
And shouting faces, while they shouted, freeze
Into black, bony masks. Before we knew
We're into them.... 'Swine!'—'Die, then'—'That's for you.'

28

"The next that I remember was a lull
And sated pause. I saw an old, old man
Lying before my feet with shattered skull
And both my arms dripped red. And then came Bran
And at his heels a hundred murderers ran,
With prisoners now, clamouring to take and try them
And burn them, wedge their nails up, crucify them.

29

"God!... Once the lying spirit of a cause
With maddening words dethrones the mind of men,
They're past the reach of prayer. The eternal laws
Hate them. Their eyes will not come clean again,
But doom and strong delusion drive them then
Without ruth, without rest ... the iron laughter
Of the immortal mouths goes hooting after.

30

"And we had firebrands too. Tower after tower
Fell sheathed in thundering flame. The street was like
A furnace mouth. We had them in our power!
Then was the time to mock them and to strike,
To flay men and spit women on the pike,
Bidding them dance. Wherever the most shame
Was done the doer called on Dymer's name.

31

"Faces of men in torture ... from my mind
They will not go away. The East lay still
In darkness when we left the town behind
Flaming to light the fields. We'd had our will:
We sang, 'Oh, we will make the frost distil
From Time's grey forehead into living dew
And break whatever has been and build new.'

32
"Day found us on the border of this wood,
Blear-eyed and pale. Then the most part began
To murmur and to lag, crying for food
And shelter. But we dared not answer Bran.
Wherever in the ranks the murmur ran
He'd find it—'You, there, whispering. Up, you sneak,
Reactionary, eh? Come out and speak.'

33
"Then there'd be shrieks, a pistol shot, a cry,
And someone down. I was the third he caught.
The others pushed me out beneath his eye,
Saying, 'He's here; here, Captain.' Who'd have thought,
My old friends? But I know now. I've been taught ...
They cut away my two hands and my feet
And laughed and left me for the birds to eat.

34
"Oh, God's name! If I had my hands again
And Dymer here ... it would not be my blood
I am stronger now than he is, old with pain,
One grip would make him mine. But it's no good,
I'm dying fast. Look, Stranger, where the wood
Grows lighter. It's the morning. Stranger dear,
Don't leave me. Talk a little while. Come near."

35

But Dymer, sitting hunched with knee to chin,
Close to the dying man, answered no word.
His face was stone. There was no meaning in
His wakeful eyes. Sometimes the other stirred
And fretted, near his death; and Dymer heard,
Yet sat like one that neither hears nor sees.
And the cold east whitened beyond the trees.

CANTO V

1

Through bearded cliffs a valley has driven thus deep
Its wedge into the mountain and no more.
The faint track of the farthest-wandering sheep
Ends here, and the grey hollows at their core
Of silence feel the dulled continuous roar
Of higher streams. At every step the skies
Grow less and in their place black ridges rise.

2

Hither, long after noon, with plodding tread
And eyes on earth, grown dogged, Dymer came,
Who all the long day in the woods had fled
From the horror of those lips that screamed his name
And cursed him. Busy wonder and keen shame
Were driving him, and little thoughts like bees
Followed and pricked him on and left no ease.

3

Now, when he looked and saw this emptiness
Seven times enfolded in the idle hills,
There came a chilly pause to his distress,
A cloud of the deep world despair that fills
A man's heart like the incoming tide and kills

All pains except its own. In that broad sea
No hope, no change, and no regret can be.

4

He felt the eternal strength of the silly earth,
The unhastening circuit of the stars and sea,
The business of perpetual death and birth,
The meaningless precision. All must be
The same and still the same in each degree—
Who cared now? And he smiled and could forgive,
Believing that for sure he would not live.

5

Then, where he saw a little water run
Beneath a bush, he slept. The chills of May
Came dropping and the stars peered one by one
Out of the deepening blue, while far away
The western brightness dulled to bars of grey.
Half-way to midnight, suddenly, from dreaming
He woke wide into present horror, screaming.

6

For he had dreamt of being in the arms
Of his beloved and in quiet places;
But all at once it filled with night alarms
And rapping guns: and men with splintered faces,
—No eyes, no nose, all red—were running races
With worms along the floor. And he ran out
To find the girl and shouted: and that shout

7

Had carried him into the waking world.
There stood the concave, vast, unfriendly night,
And over him the scroll of stars unfurled.

DYMER

Then wailing like a child he rose upright
Heart-sick with desolation. The new blight
Of loss had nipt him sore, and sad self-pity
Thinking of her—then thinking of the City.

8

For, in each moment's thought, the deeds of Bran,
The burning and the blood and his own shame,
Would tease him into madness till he ran
For refuge to the thought of her; whence came
Utter and endless loss—no, not a name,
Not a word, nothing left—himself alone
Crying amid that valley of old stone,

9

"How soon it all ran out! And I suppose
They, they up there, the old contriving powers,
They knew it all the time—for someone knows
And waits and watches till we pluck the flowers,
Then leaps. So soon—my store of happy hours
All gone before I knew. I have expended
My whole wealth in a day. It's finished, ended.

10

"And nothing left. Can it be possible
That joy flows through and, when the course is run,
It leaves no change, no mark on us to tell
Its passing? And as poor as we've begun
We end the richest day? What we have won,
Can it all die like this?... Joy flickers on
The razor-edge of the present and is gone.

11

"What have I done to bear upon my name

C. S. Lewis

The curse of Bran? I was not of his crew,
Nor any man's. And Dymer has the blame—
What have I done? Wronged whom? I never knew.
What's Bran to me? I had my deed to do
And ran out by myself, alone and free.
—Why should earth sing with joy and not for me?

12
"Ah, but the earth never did sing for joy....
There is a glamour on the leaf and flower
And April comes and whistles to a boy
Over white fields: and, beauty has such power
Upon us, he believes her in that hour,
For who could not believe? Can it be false,
All that the blackbird says and the wind calls?

13
"What have I done? No living thing I made
Nor wished to suffer harm. I sought my good
Because the spring was gloriously arrayed
And the blue eyebright misted all the wood.
Yet to obey that springtime and my blood,
This was to be unarmed and off my guard
And gave God time to hit once and hit hard.

14
"The men build right who made that City of ours,
They knew their world. A man must crouch to face
Infinite malice, watching at all hours,
Shut nature out—give her no moment's space
For entry. The first needs of all our race
Are walls, a den, a cover. Traitor I
Who first ran out beneath the open sky.

43

DYMER

15

"Our fortress and fenced place I made to fall,
I slipt the sentries and let in the foe.
I have lost my brothers and my love and all.
Nothing is left but me. Now let me go.
I have seen the world stripped naked and I know.
Great God, take back your world. I will have none
Of all your glittering gauds but death alone."

16

Meanwhile the earth swung round in hollow night.
Souls without number in all nations slept,
Snug on her back, safe speeding towards the light,
Hours tolled, and in damp woods the night beast crept,
And over the long seas the watch was kept
In black ships, twinkling onward, green and red:
Always the ordered stars moved overhead.

17

And no one knew that Dymer in his scales
Had weighed all these and found them nothing worth.
Indifferently the dawn that never fails
Troubled the east of night with gradual birth,
Whispering a change of colours on cold earth,
And a bird woke, then two. The sunlight ran
Along the hills and yellow day began.

18

But stagnant gloom clung in the valley yet;
Hills crowded out a third part of the sky,
Black-looking, and the boulders dripped with wet:
No bird sang. Dymer, shivering, heaved a sigh
And yawned and said: "It's cruel work to die
Of hunger"; and again, with cloudy breath

C. S. Lewis

Blown between chattering teeth, "It's a bad death."

19
He crouched and clasped his hands about his knees
And hugged his own limbs for the pitiful sense
Of homeliness they had—familiars these,
This body, at least, his own, his last defence.
But soon his morning misery drove him thence,
Eating his heart, to wander as chance led
On, upward, to the narrowing gulley's head.

20
The cloud lay on the nearest mountain-top
As from a giant's chimney smoking there,
But Dymer took no heed. Sometimes he'd stop,
Sometimes he hurried faster, as despair
Pricked deeper, and cried out: "Even now, somewhere,
Bran with his crew's at work. They rack, they burn,
And there's no help in me. I've served their turn."

21
Meanwhile the furrowed fog rolled down ahead,
Long tatters of its vanguard smearing round
The bases of the crags. Like cobweb shed
Down the deep combes it dulled the tinkling sound
Of water on the hills. The spongy ground
Faded three yards ahead: then nearer yet
Fell the cold wreathes, the white depth gleaming wet.

22
Then after a long time the path he trod
Led downward. Then all suddenly it dipped
Far steeper, and yet steeper, with smooth sod.
He was half running now. A stone that slipped

DYMER

Beneath him, rattled headlong down: he tripped,
Stumbled and clutched—then panic, and no hope
To stop himself, once lost upon that slope.

23
And faster, ever faster, and his eye
Caught tree-tops far below. The nightmare feeling
Had gripped him. He was screaming: and the sky
Seemed hanging upside down. Then struggling, reeling,
With effort beyond thought he hung half kneeling,
Halted one saving moment With wild will
He clawed into the hillside and lay still,

24
Half hanging on both arms. His idle feet
Dangled and found no hold. The moor lay wet
Against him and he sweated with the heat
Of terror, all alive. His teeth were set.
"By God, I will not die," said he. "Not yet."
Then slowly, slowly, with enormous strain,
He heaved himself an inch: then heaved again,

25
Till saved and spent he lay. He felt indeed
It was the big, round world beneath his breast,
The mother planet proven at his need.
The shame of glad surrender stood confessed,
He cared not for his boasts. This, this was best,
This giving up of all. He need not strive;
He panted, he lay still, he was alive.

26
And now his eyes were closed. Perhaps he slept
Lapt in unearthly quiet—never knew

How bit by bit the fog's white rearguard crept
Over the crest and faded, and the blue
First brightening at the zenith trembled through
And deepening shadows took a sharper form
Each moment, and the sandy earth grew warm.

27

Yet, dreaming of blue skies, in dream he heard
The pure voice of a lark that seemed to send
Its song from heights beyond all height That bird
Sang out of heaven, "The world will never end,"
Sang from the gates of heaven, "Will never end,"
Sang till it seemed there was no other thing
But bright space and one voice set there to sing.

28

It seemed to be the murmur and the voice
Of beings beyond number, each and all
Singing I am. Each of itself made choice
And was: whence flows the justice that men call
Divine. She keeps the great worlds lest they fall
From hour to hour, and makes the hills renew
Their ancient youth and sweetens all things through.

29

It seemed to be the low voice of the world
Brooding alone beneath the strength of things,
Murmuring of days and nights and years unfurled
Forever, and the unwearied joy that brings
Out of old fields the flowers of unborn springs,
Out of old wars and cities burned with wrong,
A splendour in the dark, a tale, a song.

30

The dream ran thin towards waking, and he knew
It was a bird's piping with no sense.
He rolled round on his back. The sudden blue,
Quivering with light, hard, cloudless and intense,
Shone over him. The lark still sounded thence
And stirred him at the heart Some spacious thought
Was passing by too gently to be caught.

31

With that he thrust the damp hair from his face
And sat upright. The perilous cliff dropped sheer
Before him, close at hand, and from his place
Listening in mountain silence he could hear
Birds crying far below. It was not fear
That took him, but strange glory, when his eye
Looked past the edge into surrounding sky.

32

He rose and stood. Then lo! the world beneath
—Wide pools that in the sun-splashed foot hills lay,
Sheep-dotted downs, soft-piled, and rolling heath,
River and shining weir and steeples grey
And the green waves of forest Far away
Distance rose heaped on distance: nearer hand,
The white roads leading down to a new land.

CANTO VI

1

The sun was high in heaven and Dymer stood
A bright speck on the endless mountain-side.
Till, blossom after blossom, that rich mood
Faded and truth rolled homeward, like a tide
Before whose edge the weak soul fled to hide
In vain, with ostrich head, through many a shape

Of coward fancy, whimpering for escape.

2

But only for a moment; then his soul
Took the full swell and heaved a dripping prow
Clear of the shattering wave-crest. He was whole.
No veils should hide the truth, no truth should cow
The dear self-pitying heart "I'll babble now
No longer," Dymer said. "I'm broken in.
Pack up the dreams and let the life begin."

3

With this he turned. "I must have food to-day,"
He muttered. Then among the cloudless hills
By winding tracks he sought the downward way
And followed the steep course of tumbling rills
—Came to the glens the wakening mountain fills
In springtime with the echoing splash and shock
Of waters leaping cold from rock to rock.

4

And still, it seemed, that lark with its refrain
Sang in the sky and wind was in his hair
And hope at heart. Then once, and once again,
He heard a gun fired off. It broke the air
As a stone breaks a pond, and everywhere
The dry crags echoed clear: and at the sound
Once a big bird rose whirring from the ground.

5

In half an hour he reached the level land
And followed the field-paths and crossed the stiles,
Then looked and saw, near by, on his left hand
An old house, folded round with billowy piles

Of dark yew hedge. The moss was on the tiles,
The pigeons in the yard, and in the tower
A clock that had no hands and told no hour.

6

He hastened. In warm waves the garden scent
Came stronger at each stride. The mountain breeze
Was gone. He reached the gates; then in he went
And seemed to lose the sky—such weight of trees
Hung overhead. He heard the noise of bees
And saw, far off, in the blue shade between
The windless elms, one walking on the green.

7

It was a mighty man whose beardless face
Beneath grey hair shone out so large and mild
It made a sort of moonlight in the place.
A dreamy desperation, wistful-wild,
Showed in his glance and gait: yet like a child,
An Asian emperor's only child, was he
With his grave looks and bright solemnity.

8

And over him there hung the witching air,
The wilful courtesy, of the days of old.
The graces wherein idleness grows fair;
And somewhat in his sauntering walk he rolled
And toyed about his waist with seals of gold,
Or stood to ponder often in mid-stride,
Tilting his heavy head upon one side.

9

When Dymer had called twice, he turned his eye:
Then, coming out of silence (as a star

All in one moment slips into the sky
Of evening, yet we feel it comes from far),
He said, "Sir, you are welcome. Few there are
That come my way": and in huge hands he pressed
Dymer's cold hand and bade him in to rest.

10
"How did you find this place out? Have you heard
My gun? It was but now I killed a lark."
"What Sir," said Dymer, "shoot the singing bird?"
"Sir," said the man, "they sing from dawn till dark,
And interrupt my dreams too long. But hark...
Another? Did you hear no singing? No?
It was my fancy, then ... pray, let it go.

11
"From here you see my garden's only flaw.
Stand here, Sir, at the dial." Dymer stood.
The Master pointed; then he looked and saw
How hedges and the funeral quietude
Of black trees fringed the garden like a wood,
And only, in one place, one gap that showed
The blue side of the hills, the white hill-road.

12
"I have planted fir and larch to fill the gap,"
He said, "because this too makes war upon
The art of dream. But by some great mishap
Nothing I plant will grow there. We pass on....
The sunshine of the afternoon is gone.
Let us go in. It draws near time to sup
—I hate the garden till the moon is up."

DYMER

13

They passed from the hot lawn into the gloom
And coolness of the porch: then, past a door
That opened with no noise, into a room
Where green leaves choked the window and the floor
Sank lower than the ground. A tattered store
Of brown books met the eye: a crystal ball:
And masks with empty eyes along the wall.

14

Then Dymer sat, but knew not how nor where,
And supper was set out before these two,
—He saw not how—with silver old and rare
But tarnished. And he ate and never knew
What meats they were. At every bite he grew
More drowsy and let slide his crumbling will.
The Master at his side was talking still.

15

And all his talk was tales of magic words
And of the nations in the clouds above,
Astral and aerish tribes who fish for birds
With angles. And by history he could prove
How chosen spirits from earth had won their love,
As Arthur, or Usheen: and to their isle
Went Helen for the sake of a Greek smile.

16

And ever in his talk he mustered well
His texts and strewed old authors round the way,
"Thus Wierus writes," and "Thus the Hermetics tell,"
"This was Agrippa's view," and "Others say
With Cardan," till he had stolen quite away
Dymer's dull wits and softly drawn apart

C. S. Lewis

The ivory gates of hope that change the heart.

17
Dymer was talking now. Now Dymer told
Of his own love and losing, drowsily.
The Master leaned towards him, "Was it cold,
This spirit, to the touch?"—"No, Sir, not she,"
Said Dymer. And his host: "Why this must be
Aethereal, not aereal! Oh my soul,
Be still ... but wait. Tell on, Sir, tell the whole."

18
Then Dymer told him of the beldam too,
The old, old, matriarchal dreadfulness.
Over the Master's face a shadow drew,
He shifted in his chair and "Yes" and "Yes,"
He murmured twice. "I never looked for less!
Always the same ... that frightful woman shape
Besets the dream-way and the soul's escape."

19
But now when Dymer made to talk of Bran,
A huge indifference fell upon his host,
Patient and wandering-eyed. Then he began,
"Forgive me. You are young. What helps us most
Is to find out again that heavenly ghost
Who loves you. For she was a ghost, and you
In that place where you met were ghostly too.

20
"Listen! for I can launch you on the stream
Will roll you to the shores of her own land....
I could be sworn you never learned to dream,
But every night you take with careless hand

DYMER

What chance may bring? I'll teach you to command
The comings and the goings of your spirit
Through all that borderland which dreams inherit.

21

"You shall have hauntings suddenly. And often,
When you forget, when least you think of her
(For so you shall forget) a light will soften
Over the evening woods. And in the stir
Of morning dreams (oh, I will teach you, Sir)
There'll come a sound of wings. Or you shall be
Waked in the midnight murmuring, 'It was she.'"

22

"No, no," said Dymer, "not that way. I seem
To have slept for twenty years. Now—while I shake
Out of my eyes that dust of burdening dream,
Now when the long clouds tremble ripe to break
And the far hills appear, when first I wake,
Still blinking, struggling towards the world of men,
And longing—would you turn me back again?

23

"Dreams? I have had my dream too long. I thought
The sun rose for my sake. I ran down blind
And dancing to the abyss. Oh, Sir, I brought
Boy-laughter for a gift to Gods who find
The martyr's soul too soft But that's behind.
I'm waking now. They broke me. All ends thus
Always—and we're for them, not they for us.

24

"And she—she was no dream. It would be waste
To seek her there, the living in that den

Of lies." The Master smiled. "You are in haste!
For broken dreams the cure is, Dream again
And deeper. If the waking world, and men,
And nature marred your dream—so much the worse
For a crude world beneath its primal curse."

25

—"Ah, but you do not know! Can dreams do this,
Pluck out blood-guiltiness upon the shore
Of memory—and undo what's done amiss,
And bid the thing that has been be no more?"
—"Sir, it is only dreams unlock that door,"
He answered with a shrug. "What would you have?
In dreams the thrice-proved coward can feel brave.

26

"In dreams the fool is free from scorning voices.
Grey-headed whores are virgin there again.
Out of the past dream brings long-buried choices,
All in a moment snaps the tenfold chain
That life took years in forging. There the stain
Of oldest sins—how do the good words go?—
Though they were scarlet, shall be white as snow."

27

Then, drawing near, when Dymer did not speak,
"My little son," said he, "your wrong and right
Are also dreams: fetters to bind the weak
Faster to phantom earth and blear the sight.
Wake into dreams, into the larger light
That quenches these frail stars. They will not know
Earth's bye-laws in the land to which you go."

DYMER

28

—"I must undo my sins,"—"An earthly law,
And, even in earth, the child of yesterday.
Throw down your human pity; cast your awe
Behind you; put repentance all away.
Home to the elder depths! for never they
Supped with the stars who dared not slough behind
The last shred of earth's holies from their mind."

29

"Sir," answered Dymer, "I would be content
To drudge in earth, easing my heart's disgrace,
Counting a year's long service lightly spent
If once at the year's end I saw her face
Somewhere, being then most weary, in some place
I looked not for that joy—or heard her near
Whispering, 'Yet courage, friend,' for one more year."

30

"Pish," said the Master. "Will you have the truth?
You think that virtue saves? Her people care
For the high heart and idle hours of youth;
For these they will descend our lower air,
Not virtue. You would nerve your arm and bear
Your burden among men! Look to it, child:
By virtue's self vision can be defiled.

31

"You will grow full of pity and the love of men,
And toil until the morning moisture dries
Out of your heart. Then once, or once again
It may be you will find her: but your eyes
Soon will be grown too dim. The task that lies
Next to your hand will hide her. You shall be

56

C. S. Lewis

The child of earth and gods you shall not see."

32
Here suddenly he ceased. Tip-toes he went.
A bolt clicked—then the window creaked ajar,
And out of the wet world the hedgerow scent
Came floating; and the dark without one star
Nor shape of trees nor sense of near and far,
The undimensioned night and formless skies
Were there, and were the Master's great allies.

33
"I am very old," he said. "But if the time
We suffered in our dreams were counting age,
I have outlived the ocean and my prime
Is with me to this day. Years cannot gauge
The dream-life. In the turning of a page,
Dozing above my book, I have lived through
More ages than the lost Lemuria knew.

34
"I am not mortal. Were I doomed to die
This hour, in this half-hour I interpose
A thousand years of dream: and, those gone by,
As many more, and in the last of those,
Ten thousand—ever journeying towards a close
That I shall never reach: for time shall flow,
Wheel within wheel, interminably slow.

35
"And you will drink my cup and go your way
Into the valley of dreams. You have heard the call.
Come hither and escape. Why should you stay?
Earth is a sinking ship, a house whose wall

Is tottering while you sweep; the roof will fall
Before the work is done. You cannot mend it.
Patch as you will, at last the rot must end it."

36
Then Dymer lifted up his heavy head
Like Atlas on broad shoulders bearing up
The insufferable globe. "I had not said,"
He mumbled, "Never said I'd taste the cup.
What, is it this you give me? Must I sup?
Oh lies, all lies.... Why did you kill the lark?
Guide me the cup to lip ... it is so dark."

CANTO VII

1
The host had trimmed his lamp. The downy moth
Came from the garden. Where the lamplight shed
Its circle of smooth white upon the cloth,
Down mid the rinds of fruit and broken bread,
Upon his sprawling arms lay Dymer's head;
And often, as he dreamed, he shifted place,
Muttering and showing half his drunken face.

2
The beating stillness of the dead of night
Flooded the room. The dark and sleepy powers
Settled upon the house and filled it quite;
Far from the roads it lay, from belfry towers
And hen-roosts, in a world of folded flowers,
Buried in loneliest fields where beasts that love
The silence through the unrustled hedgegrows move.

3
Now from the Master's lips there breathed a sigh

C. S. Lewis

As of a man released from some control
That wronged him. Without aim his wandering eye,
Unsteadied and unfixed, began to roll.
His lower lip dropped loose. The informing soul
Seemed fading from his face. He laughed out loud
Once only: then looked round him, hushed and cowed.

4

Then, summoning all himself, with tightened lip,
With desperate coolness and attentive air,
He touched between his thumb and finger tip,
Each in its turn, the four legs of his chair,
Then back again in haste—there!—that one there
Had been forgotten ... once more! ... safer now;
That's better! and he smiled and cleared his brow.

5

Yet this was but a moment's ease. Once more
He glanced about him like a startled hare,
His big eyes bulged with horror. As before,
Quick!—to the touch that saves him. But despair
Is nearer by one step; and in his chair
Huddling he waits. He knows that they'll come strong
Again and yet again and all night long;

6

And after this night comes another night
—Night after night until the worst of all.
And now too even the noonday and the light
Let through the horrors. Oh, could he recall
The deep sleep and the dreams that used to fall
Around him for the asking. But, somehow,
Something's amiss ... sleep comes so rarely now.

DYMER

7

Then, like the dog returning to its vomit,
He staggered to the bookcase to renew
Yet once again the taint he had taken from it,
And shuddered as he went. But horror drew
His feet, as joy draws others. There in view
Was his strange heaven and his far stranger hell,
His secret lust, his soul's dark citadel:—

8

Old Theogmagia, Demonology,
Cabbala, Chemic Magic, Book of the Dead,
Damning Hermetic rolls that none may see
Save the already damned—such grules are bred
From minds that lose the Spirit and seek instead
For spirits in the dust of dead men's error,
Buying the joys of dream with dreamland terror.

9

This lost soul looked them over one and all
Now sickened at the heart's root; for he knew
This night was one of those when he would fall
And scream alone (such things they made him do)
And roll upon the floor. The madness grew
Wild at his breast, but still his brain was clear
That he could watch the moment coming near.

10

But, ere it came, he heard a sound, half groan,
Half muttering, from the table. Like a child
Caught unawares that thought it was alone,
He started as in guilt. His gaze was wild,
Yet pitiably with all his will he smiled,
—So strong is shame, even then. And Dymer stirred,

C. S. Lewis

Now waking, and looked up and spoke one word:

11
"Water!" he said. He was too dazed to see
What hell-wrung face looked down, what shaking hand
Poured out the draught. He drank it thirstily
And held the glass for more. "Your land ... your land
Of dreams," he said. "All lies!... I understand
More than I did. Yes, water. I've the thirst
Of hell itself. Your magic's all accursed."

12
When he had drunk again he rose and stood,
Pallid and cold with sleep. "By God," he said,
"You did me wrong to send me to that wood.
I sought a living spirit and found instead
Bogys and wraiths." The Master raised his head
Calm as a sage and answered, "Are you mad?
Come, sit you down. Tell me what dream you had."

13
—"I dreamed about a wood ... an autumn red
Of beech-trees big as mountains. Down between—
The first thing that I saw—a clearing spread,
Deep down, oh, very deep. Like some ravine
Or like a well it sank, that forest green
Under its weight of forest—more remote
Than one ship in a landlocked sea afloat.

14
"Then through the narrowed sky some heavy bird
Would flap its way, a stillness more profound
Following its languid wings. Sometimes I heard
Far off in the long woods with quiet sound

DYMER

The sudden chestnut thumping to the ground,
Or the dry leaf that drifted past upon
Its endless loiter earthward and was gone.

15
"Then next ... I heard twigs splintering on my right
And rustling in the thickets. Turning there
I watched. Out of the foliage came in sight
The head and blundering shoulders of a bear,
Glistening in sable black, with beady stare
Of eyes towards me, and no room to fly
—But padding soft and slow the beast came by.

16
"And—mark their flattery—stood and rubbed his flank
Against me. On my shaken legs I felt
His heart beat. And my hand that stroked him sank
Wrist-deep upon his shoulder in soft pelt.
Yes ... and across my spirit as I smelt
The wild thing's scent, a new, sweet wildness ran
Whispering of Eden-fields long lost by man.

17
"So far was well. But then came emerald birds
Singing about my head. I took my way
Sauntering the cloistered woods. Then came the herds,
The roebuck and the fallow deer at play
Trooping to nose my hand. All this, you say,
Was sweet? Oh sweet!... do you think I could not see
That beasts and wood were nothing else but me?

18
"... That I was making everything I saw,
Too sweet, far too well fitted to desire

To be a living thing? Those forests draw
No sap from the kind earth: the solar fire
And soft rain feed them not: that fairy brier
Pricks not: the birds sing sweetly in that brake
Not for their own delight but for my sake!

19

"It is a world of sad, cold, heartless stuff,
Like a bought smile, no joy in it."—"But stay;
Did you not find your lady?"—"Sure enough!
I still had hopes till then. The autumn day
Was westering, the long shadows crossed my way,
When over daisies folded for the night
Beneath rook-gathering elms she came in sight."

20

—"Was she not fair?"—"So beautiful, she seemed
Almost a living soul. But every part
Was what I made it—all that I had dreamed—
No more, no less: the mirror of my heart,
Such things as boyhood feigns beneath the smart
Of solitude and spring. I was deceived
Almost. In that first moment I believed.

21

"For a big, brooding rapture, tense as fire
And calm as a first sleep had soaked me through
Without thought, without word, without desire....
Meanwhile above our heads the deepening blue
Burnished the gathering stars. Her sweetness drew
A veil before my eyes. The minutes passed
Heavy like loaded vines. She spoke at last.

DYMER

22

"She said, for this land only did men love
The shadow-lands of earth. All our disease
Of longing, all the hopes we fabled of,
Fortunate islands or Hesperean seas
Or woods beyond the West, were but the breeze
That blew from off those shores: one farspent breath
That reached even to the world of change and death.

23

"She told me I had journeyed home at last
Into the golden age and the good countrie
That had been always there. She bade me cast
My cares behind forever:—on her knee
Worshipped me, lord and love—oh, I can see
Her red lips even now! Is it not wrong
That men's delusions should be made so strong?

24

"For listen, I was so besotted now
She made me think that I was somehow seeing
The very core of truth ... I felt somehow,
Beyond all veils, the inward pulse of being.
Thought was enslaved, but oh, it felt like freeing
And draughts of larger air. It is too much!
Who can come through untainted from that touch?

25

"There I was nearly wrecked. But mark the rest:
She went too fast. Soft to my arms she came.
The robe slipped from her shoulder. The smooth breast
Was bare against my own. She shone like flame
Before me in the dusk, all love, all shame—
Faugh!—and it was myself. But all was well,

64

C. S. Lewis

For, at the least, that moment snapped the spell.

26

"As when you light a candle, the great gloom
Which was the unbounded night, sinks down, compressed
To four white walls in one familiar room,
So the vague joy shrank wilted in my breast
And narrowed to one point, unmasked, confessed;
Fool's paradise was gone: instead was there
King Lust with his black, sudden, serious stare.

27

"That moment in a cloud among the trees
Wild music and the glare of torches came.
On sweated faces, on the prancing knees
Of shaggy satyrs fell the smoky flame,
On ape and goat and crawlers without name,
On rolling breast, black eyes and tossing hair,
On old bald-headed witches, lean and bare.

28

"They beat the devilish tom-tom rub-a-dub;
Lunging, leaping, in unwieldy romp,
Singing Cotytto and Beelzebub,
With devil dancers mask and phallic pomp,
Torn raw with briers and caked from many a swamp
They came, among the wild flowers dripping blood
And churning the green mosses into mud.

29

"They sang, 'Return! Return! We are the lust
That was before the world and still shall be
When your last law is trampled into dust,
We are the mother swamp, the primal sea

DYMER

Whence the dry land appeared. Old, old are we.
It is but a return ... it's nothing new,
Easy as slipping on a well-worn shoe.'

30
"And then there came warm mouths and finger-tips
Preying upon me, whence I could not see,
Then ... a huge face, low browed, with swollen lips
Crooning 'I am not beautiful as she,
But I'm the older love; you shall love me
Far more than Beauty's self. You have been ours
Always. We are the world's most ancient powers.'

31
"First flatterer and then bogy—like a dream!
Sir, are you listening? Do you also know
How close to the soft laughter comes the scream
Down yonder?" But his host cried sharply, "No.
Leave me alone. Why will you plague me? Go!
Out of my house! Begone."—"With all my heart,"
Said Dymer. "But one word before we part."

32
He paused, and in his cheek the anger burned:
Then turning to the table, he poured out
More water. But before he drank he turned—
Then leaped back to the window with a shout
For there—it was no dream—beyond all doubt
He saw the Master crouch with levelled gun
Cackling in maniac voice, "Run, Dymer, run!"

33
He ducked and sprang far out. The starless night
On the wet lawn closed round him every way.

Then came the gun-crack and the splash of light
Vanished as soon as seen. Cool garden clay
Slid from his feet. He had fallen and he lay
Face downward among leaves—then up and on
Through branch and leaf till sense and breath were gone.

CANTO VIII

1

When next he found himself no house was there,
No garden and great trees. Beside a lane
In grass he lay. Now first he was aware
That, all one side, his body glowed with pain:
And the next moment and the next again
Was neither less nor more. Without a pause
It clung like a great beast with fastened claws;

2

That for a time he could not frame a thought
Nor know himself for self, nor pain for pain,
Till moment added on to moment taught
The new, strange art of living on that plane,
Taught how the grappled soul must still remain,
Still choose and think and understand beneath
The very grinding of the ogre's teeth.

3

He heard the wind along the hedges sweep,
The quarter striking from a neighbouring tower.
About him was the weight of the world's sleep;
Within, the thundering pain. That quiet hour
Heeded it not. It throbbed, it raged with power
Fit to convulse the heavens; and at his side
The soft peace drenched the meadows far and wide.

DYMER

4

The air was cold, the earth was cold with dew,
The hedge behind him dark as ink. But now
The clouds broke and a paler heaven showed through
Spacious with sudden stars, breathing somehow
The sense of change to slumbering lands. A cow
Coughed in the fields behind. The puddles showed
Like pools of sky amid the darker road.

5

And he could see his own limbs faintly white
And the blood black upon them. Then by chance
He turned ... and it was strange; there at his right
He saw a woman standing, and her glance
Met his: and at the meeting his deep trance
Changed not, and while he looked the knowledge grew
She was not of the old life but the new.

6

"Who is it?" he said. "The loved one, the long lost."
He stared upon her. "Truly?"—"Truly indeed."
"Oh, lady, you come late. I am tempest-tossed,
Broken and wrecked. I am dying. Look, I bleed.
Why have you left me thus and given no heed
To all my prayers?—left me to be the game
Of all deceits?"—"You should have asked my name."

7

—"What are you, then?" But to his sudden cry
She did not answer. When he had thought awhile
He said: "How can I tell it is no lie?
It may be one more phantom to beguile
The brain-sick dreamer with its harlot smile."
"I have not smiled," she said. The neighbouring bell

Tolled out another quarter. Silence fell.

8

And after a long pause he spoke again:
"Leave me," he said. "Why do you watch with me?
You do not love me. Human tears and pain
And hoping for the things that cannot be,
And blundering in the night where none can see,
And courage with cold back against the wall,
You do not understand."—"I know them all.

9

"The gods themselves know pain, the eternal forms.
In realms beyond the reach of cloud, and skies
Nearest the ends of air, where come no storms
Nor sound of earth, I have looked into their eyes
Peaceful and filled with pain beyond surmise,
Filled with an ancient woe man cannot reach
One moment though in fire; yet calm their speech."

10

"Then these," said Dymer, "were the world I wooed ...
These were the holiness of flowers and grass
And desolate dews ... these, the eternal mood
Blowing the eternal theme through men that pass.
I called myself their lover—I that was
Less fit for that long service than the least
Dull, workday drudge of men or faithful beast.

11

"Why do they lure to them such spirits as mine,
The weak, the passionate, and the fool of dreams?
When better men go safe and never pine
With whisperings at the heart, soul-sickening gleams

Of infinite desire, and joy that seems
The promise of full power? For it was they,
The gods themselves that led me on this way.

12

"Give me the truth! I ask not now for pity.
When gods call, can the following them be sin?
Was it false light that lured me from the City?
Where was the path—without it or within?
Must it be one blind throw to lose or win?
Has heaven no voice to help? Must things of dust
Guess their own way in the dark?" She said, "They must."

13

Another silence: then he cried in wrath,
"You came in human shape, in sweet disguise
Wooing me, lurking for me in my path,
Hid your eternal cold with woman's eyes,
Snared me with shows of love—and all was lies."
She answered, "For our kind must come to all
If bidden, but in the shape for which they call."

14

"What," answered Dymer. "Do you change and sway
To serve us, as the obedient planets spin
About the sun? Are you but potter's clay
For us to mould—unholy to our sin
And holy to the holiness within?"
She said, "Waves fall on many an unclean shore,
Yet the salt seas are holy as before.

15

"Our nature is no purer for the saint
That worships, nor from him that uses ill

Our beauty, can we suffer any taint.
As from the first we were, so are we still:
With incorruptibles the mortal will
Corrupts itself, and clouded eyes will make
Darkness within from beams they cannot take."

16

"Well ... it is well," said Dymer. "If I have used
The embreathing spirit amiss ... what would have been
The strength of all my days I have refused
And plucked the stalk, too hasty, in the green,
Trusted the good for best, and having seen
Half-beauty, or beauty's fringe, the lowest stair,
The common incantation, worshipped there."

17

But presently he cried in his great pain,
"If I had loved a beast it would repay,
But I have loved the Spirit and loved in vain.
Now let me die ... ah, but before the way
Is ended quite, in the last hour of day,
Is there no word of comfort, no one kiss
Of human love? Does it all end in this?"

18

She answered, "Never ask of life and death.
Uttering these names you dream of wormy clay
Or of surviving ghosts. This withering breath
Of words is the beginning of decay
In truth, when truth grows cold and pines away
Among the ancestral images. Your eyes
First see her dead: and more, the more she dies.

19

DYMER

"You are still dreaming, dreams you shall forget
When you have cast your fetters, far from here.
Go forth, the journey is not ended yet.
You have seen Dymer dead and on the bier
More often than you dream and dropped no tear,
You have slain him every hour. Think not at all
Of death lest into death by thought you fall."

20
He turned to question her, then looked again,
And lo! the shape was gone. The darkness lay
Heavy as yet and a cold, shifting rain
Fell with the breeze that springs before the day.
It was an hour death loves. Across the way
The clock struck once again. He saw near by
The black shape of the tower against the sky.

21
Meanwhile above the torture and the riot
Of leaping pulse and nerve that shot with pain,
Somewhere aloof and poised in spectral quiet
His soul was thinking on. The dizzied brain
Scarce seemed her organ: link by link the chain
That bound him to the flesh was loosening fast
And the new life breathed in unmoved and vast.

22
"It was like this," he thought. "Like this, or worse
For him that I found bleeding in the wood ...
Blessings upon him ... there I learned the curse
That rests on Dymer's name, and truth was good.
He has forgotten now the fire and blood,
He has forgotten that there was a man
Called Dymer. He knows not himself nor Bran.

23

"How long have I been moved at heart in vain
About this Dymer, thinking this was I ...
Why did I follow close his joy and pain
More than another man's? For he will die,
The little cloud will vanish and the sky
Reigns as before. The stars remain and earth
And Man, as in the years before my birth.

24

"There was a Dymer once who worked and played
About the City; I sloughed him off and ran.
There was a Dymer in the forest glade
Ranting alone, skulking the fates of man.
I cast him also, and a third began
And he too died. But I am none of those.
Is there another still to die.... Who knows?"

25

Then in his pain, half wondering what he did,
He made to struggle towards that belfried place.
And groaning down the sodden bank he slid
And groaning in the lane he felt his trace
Of bloodied mire: then halted with his face
Upwards, towards the gateway, breathing hard
—An old lych-gate before a burial-yard.

26

He looked within. Between the huddling crosses,
Over the slanted tombs and sunken slate
Spread the deep quiet grass and humble mosses,
A green and growing darkness, drenched of late,
Smelling of earth and damp. He reached the gate
With failing hand. "I will rest here," he said,

"And the long grass will cool my burning head."

CANTO IX

1

Even as he heard the wicket clash behind
Came a great wind beneath that seemed to tear
The solid graves apart; and deaf and blind
Whirled him upright like smoke, through towering air.
Whose levels were as steps of a sky stair.
The parching cold roughened his throat with thirst
And pricked him at the heart. This was the first.

2

And as he soared into the next degree,
Suddenly all around him he could hear
Sad strings that fretted inconsolably
And ominous horns that blew both far and near.
There broke his human heart, and his last tear
Froze scalding on his chin. But while he heard
He shot like a sped dart into the third.

3

And its first stroke of silence could destroy
The spring of tears forever and compress
From off his lips the curved bow of the boy
Forever. The sidereal loneliness
Received him, where no journeying leaves the less
Still to be journeyed through: but everywhere,
Fast though you fly, the centre still is there.

4

And here the well-worn fabric of our life,
Fell from him. Hope and purpose were cut short,
—Even the blind trust that reaches in mid-strife

74

C. S. Lewis

Towards some heart of things. Here blew the mort
For the world spirit herself. The last support
Was fallen away—Himself, one spark of soul,
Swam in unbroken void. He was the whole,

5

And wailing: "Why hast Thou forsaken me?
Was there no world at all, but only I
Dreaming of gods and men?" Then suddenly
He felt the wind no more: he seemed to fly
Faster than light but free; and scaled the sky
In his own strength—as if a falling stone
Should wake to find the world's will was its own.

6

And on the instant, straight before his eyes
He looked and saw a sentry shape that stood
Leaning upon its spear, with hurrying skies
Behind it and a moonset red as blood.
Upon its head were helmet and mailed hood
And shield upon its arm and sword at thigh,
All black and pointed sharp against the sky.

7

Then came the clink of metal, the dry sound
Of steel on rock, and challenge: "Who comes here?"
And as he heard it, Dymer at one bound
Stood in the stranger's shadow, with the spear
Between them. And his human face came near
That larger face. "What watch is this you keep?"
Said Dymer, "On the edge of such a deep."

8

And answer came, "I watch both night and day

This frontier ... there are beasts of the upper air
As beasts of the deep sea ... one walks this way
Night after night, far scouring from his lair,
Chewing the cud of lusts which are despair
And fill not, while his mouth gapes dry for bliss
That never was."—"What kind of beast is this?"

9

"A kind of things escaped that have no home,
Hunters of men. They love the spring uncurled,
The will worn down, the wearied hour. They come
At night-time when the mask is off the world
And the soul's gate ill-locked and the flag furled
—Then, softly, a pale swarm, and in disguise
Flit past the drowsy watchman, small as flies."

10

"I'll see this aerish beast whereof you speak.
I'll share the watch with you."—"Nay, little One,
Begone. You are of earth. The flesh is weak...."
—"What is the flesh to me? My course is run,
All but some deed still waiting to be done,
Some moment I may rise on, as the boat
Lifts with the lifting tide and steals afloat.

11

"You are a spirit, and it is well with you,
But I am come out of great folly and shame,
The sack of cities, wrongs I must undo....
But tell me of the beast, and whence it came;
Who were its sire and dam? What is its name?"
—"It is my kin. All monsters are the brood
Of heaven and earth, and mixed with holy blood."

12
—"How can this be?"—"My son, sit here awhile.
There is a lady in that primal place
Where I was born, who with her ancient smile
Made glad the sons of heaven. She loved to chase
The springtime round the world. To all your race
She was a sudden quivering in the wood
Or a new thought springing in solitude.

13
"Till, in prodigious hour, one swollen with youth,
Blind from new broken prison, knowing not
Himself nor her, nor how to mate with truth,
Lay with her in a strange and secret spot,
Mortal with her immortal, and begot
This walker-in-the-night."—"But did you know
This mortal's name?"—"Why ... it was long ago.

14
"And yet, I think, I bear the name in mind;
It was some famished boy whom tampering men
Had crippled in their chains and made him blind
Till their weak hour discovered them: and then
He broke that prison. Softly!—it comes again,
I have it. It was Dymer, Little One,
Dymer's the name. This spectre is his son."

15
Then, after silence, came an answering shout
From Dymer, glad and full: "Break off! Dismiss!
Your watch is ended and your lamp is out
Unarm, unarm. Return into your bliss.
You are relieved, Sir. I must deal with this
As in my right. For either I must slay

DYMER

This beast or else be slain before the day."

16
"So mortal and so brave?" that other said,
Smiling, and turned and looked in Dymer's eyes,
Scanning him over twice from heel to head
—Like an old sergeant's glance, grown battle wise
To know the points of men. At last, "Arise,"
He said, "and wear my arms. I can withhold
Nothing; for such an hour has been foretold."

17
Thereat, with lips as cold as the sea-surge,
He kissed the youth, and bending on one knee
Put all his armour off and let emerge
Angelic shoulders marbled gloriously
And feet like frozen speed and, plain to see,
On his wide breast dark wounds and ancient scars,
The battle honours of celestial wars.

18
Then like a squire or brother born he dressed
The young man in those plates, that dripped with cold
Upon the inside, trickling over breast
And shoulder: but without, the figured gold
Gave to the tinkling ice its jagged hold,
And the icy spear froze fast to Dymer's hand.
But where the other had stood he took his stand

19
And searched the cloudy landscape. He could see
Dim shapes like hills appearing, but the moon
Had sunk behind their backs. "When will it be?"
Said Dymer: and the other, "Soon now, soon.

For either he comes past us at night's noon
Or else between the night and the full day,
And down there, on your left, will be his way."

20

—"Swear that you will not come between us two
Nor help me by a hair's weight if I bow."
—"If you are he, if prophesies speak true,
Not heaven and all the gods can help you now.
This much I have been told, but know not how
The fight will end. Who knows? I cannot tell."
"Sir, be content," said Dymer. "I know well."

21

Thus Dymer stood to arms, with eyes that ranged
Through aching darkness: stared upon it, so
That all things, as he looked upon them, changed
And were not as at first. But grave and slow
The larger shade went sauntering to and fro,
Humming at first the snatches of some tune
That soldiers sing, but falling silent soon.

22

Then came steps of dawn. And though they heard
No milking cry in the fields, and no cock crew,
And out of empty air no twittering bird
Sounded from neighbouring hedges, yet they knew.
Eastward the hollow blackness paled to blue,
Then blue to white: and in the West the rare,
Surviving stars blinked feebler in cold air.

23

Far beneath Dymer's feet the sad half-light
Discovering the new landscape oddly came,

And forms grown half familiar in the night
Looked strange again: no distance seemed the same.
And now he could see clear and call by name
Valleys and hills and woods. The phantoms all
Took shape, and made a world, at morning's call.

24
It was a ruinous land. The ragged stumps
Of broken trees rose out of endless clay
Naked of flower and grass: the slobbered humps
Dividing the dead pools. Against the grey
A shattered village gaped. But now the day
Was very near them and the night was past,
And Dymer understood and spoke at last.

25
"Now I have wooed and won you, bridal earth,
Beautiful world that lives, desire of men.
All that the spirit intended at my birth
This day shall be born into deed ... and then
The hard day's labour comes no more again
Forever. The pain dies. The longings cease.
The ship glides under the green arch of peace.

26
"Now drink me as the sun drinks up the mist.
This is the hour to cease in, at full flood,
That asks no gift from following years—but, hist!
Look yonder! At the corner of that wood—
Look! Look there where he comes! It shocks the blood,
The first sight, eh? Now, sentinel, stand clear
And save yourself. For God's sake come not near."

27

His full-grown spirit had moved without command
Or spur of the will. Before he knew he found
That he was leaping forward spear in hand
To where that ashen brute wheeled slowly round
Nosing, and set its ears towards the sound,
The pale and heavy brute, rough-ridged behind,
And full of eyes, clinking in scaly rind.

28
And now ten paces parted them: and here
He halted. He thrust forward his left foot,
Poising his straightened arms, and launched the spear,
And gloriously it sang. But now the brute
Lurched forward: and he saw the weapon shoot
Beyond it and fall quivering on the field.
Dymer drew out his sword and raised the shield.

29
What now, my friends? You get no more from me
Of Dymer. He goes from us. What he felt
Or saw from henceforth no man knows but he
Who has himself gone through the jungle belt
Of dying, into peace. That angel knelt
Far off and watched them close but could not see
Their battle. All was ended suddenly.

30
A leap—a cry—flurry of steel and claw,
Then silence. As before, the morning light
And the same brute crouched yonder; and he saw
Under its feet, broken and bent and white,
The ruined limbs of Dymer, killed outright
All in a moment, all his story done.
... But that same moment came the rising sun;

DYMER

31

And thirty miles to Westward, the grey cloud
Flushed into answering pink. Long shadows streamed
From every hill, and the low hanging shroud
Of mist along the valleys broke and steamed
Gold-flecked to heaven. Far off the armour gleamed
Like glass upon the dead man's back. But now
The sentinel ran forward, hand to brow,

32

And staring. For between him and the sun
He saw that country clothed with dancing flowers
Where flower had never grown; and one by one
The splintered woods, as if from April showers,
Were softening into green. In the leafy towers
Rose the cool, sudden chattering on the tongues
Of happy birds with morning in their lungs.

33

The wave of flowers came breaking round his feet,
Crocus and bluebell, primrose, daffodil
Shivering with moisture: and the air grew sweet
Within his nostrils, changing heart and will,
Making him laugh. He looked, and Dymer still
Lay dead among the flowers and pinned beneath
The brute: but as he looked he held his breath;

34

For when he had gazed hard with steady eyes
Upon the brute, behold, no brute was there,
But someone towering large against the skies,
A wing'd and sworded shape, through whom the air
Poured as through glass: and its foam-tumbled hair
Lay white about the shoulders and the whole

C. S. Lewis

Pure body brimmed with life, as a full bowl.

35
And from the distant corner of day's birth
He heard clear trumpets blowing and bells ring,
A noise of great good coming into earth
And such a music as the dumb would sing
If Balder had led back the blameless spring
With victory, with the voice of charging spears,
And in white lands long-lost Saturnian years.

www.ingramcontent.com/pod-product-compliance
Lightning Source LLC
Chambersburg PA
CBHW030524100426
42813CB00001B/140